CREEPY CONSPIRACY THEORIES

By Virginia Loh-Hagan

Disclaimer: This series focuses on the strangest of the strange. Have fun reading about strange people and things! But please do not try any of the antics in this book. Be safe and smart!

45th Parallel Press

Published in the United States of America by Cherry Lake Publishing
Ann Arbor, Michigan
www.cherrylakepublishing.com

Reading Adviser: Marla Conn MS, Ed., Literacy specialist, Read-Ability, Inc.
Book Designer: Melinda Millward

Photo Credits: © Nejron Photo / Shutterstock.com, cover; © KateMacate / Shutterstock.com, 1; © Andrey_Popov / Shutterstock.com, 5; © artisteer / iStock.com, 6; © Chad Zuber / Shutterstock.com, 7; © Janusz Pienkowski / Shutterstock.com, 8; © Pictorial Press Ltd / Alamy Stock Photo, 9; © Katherine Welles / Shutterstock.com, 10; © Mark Schwettmann / Shutterstock.com, 12; © Mayehem / iStock.com, 13; © Hank Walker / Gettyimages.com, 14; © Everett Collection Inc / Alamy Stock Photo, 15; © Anna Kucherova / Shutterstock.com, 16; © Bikeworldtravel / Shutterstock.com, 17; © Multipedia / iStock.com, 18; © adike / Shutterstock.com, 20; © photoBeard / Shutterstock.com, 21; © Chaykovsky Igor / Shutterstock.com, 22; © Artur Balytskyi / Shutterstock.com, 23; © Anyaivanova / Shutterstock.com, 24; © santosha / iStock.com, 25; © Everett Historical / Shutterstock.com, 26; © caminoel / Shutterstock.com, 27; © NASA on The Commons / flickr.com, 28; © Project Apollo Archive / flickr.com / Public Domain, 29; © NASA / nasa.gov, 30

45th Parallel Press is an imprint of Cherry Lake Publishing.

Library of Congress Cataloging-in-Publication Data

Names: Loh-Hagan, Virginia, author.
Title: Creepy conspiracy theories / by Virginia Loh-Hagan.
Description: Ann Arbor : Cherry Lake Publishing, [2018] | Series: Stranger than fiction |
    Audience: Grade 4 to 6.
Identifiers: LCCN 2017031590| ISBN 9781534107571 (hardcover) | ISBN 9781534109551 (pdf) |
    ISBN 9781534108561 (pbk.) | ISBN 9781534120549 (hosted ebook)
Subjects: LCSH: Conspiracies—Juvenile literature.
Classification: LCC HV6275 .L64 2018 | DDC 001.9—dc23
LC record available at https://lccn.loc.gov/2017031590

Printed in the United States of America
Corporate Graphics

About the Author

Dr. Virginia Loh-Hagan is an author, university professor, former classroom teacher, and curriculum designer. She thinks her dogs are conspiring to take control over the world. She lives in San Diego with her very tall husband and very naughty dogs. To learn more about her, visit www.virginialoh.com.

Table of Contents

Introduction

Some people believe in conspiracy theories. Conspiracies are secret plans. Theories are ideas. Conspiracy theories explain events differently than the accepted way. They're usually against the government. Conspiracy theorists believe the theories. They think nothing happens by accident. They think nothing is as it seems. They think others are out to get them. They think others are hiding the truth.

But there are strange conspiracy theories. And then there are really strange conspiracy theories. They're so strange that they're hard to believe. They sound like fiction. But these stories are all true!

Conspiracy theorists believe evil forces are out there.

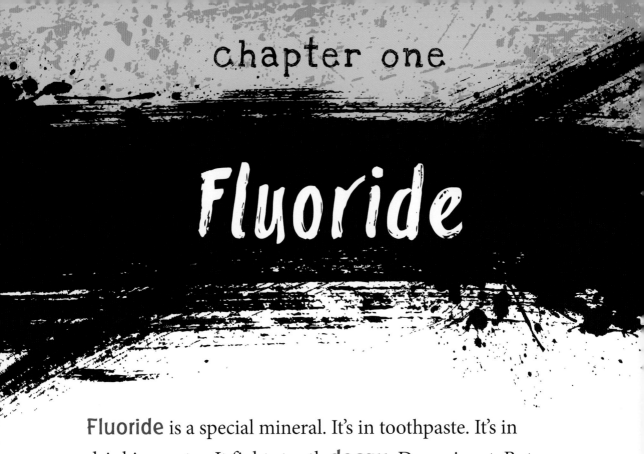

chapter one

Fluoride

Fluoride is a special mineral. It's in toothpaste. It's in drinking water. It fights tooth **decay**. Decay is rot. But some people think fluoride is bad. They think it harms our bodies.

Some theorists blame drug companies. They think drug companies are poisoning people. The companies want people to be sick. Sick people have to buy medicine. This makes money for drug companies.

Some theorists blame **communists**. Communists believe goods should be owned in common. Theorists think

6

Government officials and scientists say the amount of fluoride in water is safe.

communists want to make everyone dumb. Fluoride is how they control people's minds.

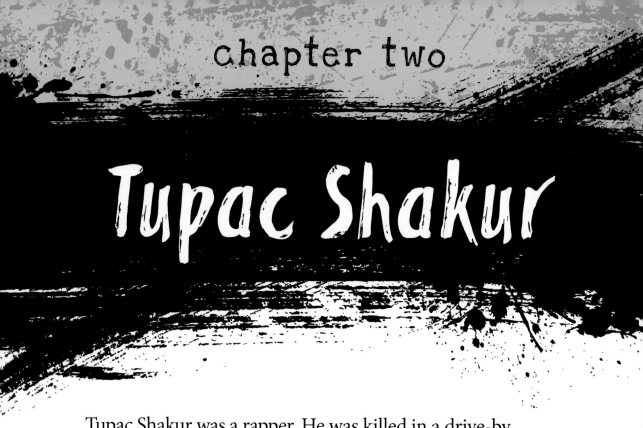

chapter two

Tupac Shakur

Tupac Shakur was a rapper. He was killed in a drive-by shooting. This happened in Las Vegas, Nevada. This happened in 1996. His killing is a mystery. There are several conspiracy theories.

Some theorists think Shakur is still alive. They think Shakur faked his death. Shakur studied Niccolò Machiavelli. Machiavelli was a famous thinker. He wrote *The Art of War*. He advised faking one's death to control an enemy. Shakur's stage name was "Makaveli."

The letters in "Makaveli" can be rearranged to read "AM ALIVE K."

Some theorists think he's hiding in Cuba. Shakur is thought to be living with his aunt.

Some theorists think the government knows where he is. They think Shakur has proof against criminals. He's thought to be in **witness** protection. A witness is someone who sees something.

Some theorists think Shakur's friends planned his killing. Suge Knight was his boss. David Kenner was his lawyer. Knight and Kenner were thought to be greedy. They were afraid of getting fired. They didn't want to lose Shakur's money.

Some theorists think Biggie Smalls had Shakur killed. Smalls was a rapper. He and Shakur competed against each other. He's thought to have paid a gang to kill Shakur.

The FBI has denied protecting Shakur.

10

Explained by Science

Scientists don't trust conspiracy theories. They admit these theories may have some truth. But as a whole, they're not true. Humans find patterns and meanings. They're uncomfortable with the unknown. They make up ideas to explain things. Conspiracy theorists may have "confirmation bias." This means they pay more attention to information that supports what they think. They ignore information that disagrees with their ideas. They see mistakes as cover-ups. They don't like being wrong. Experts say that conspiracy theorists are more likely to be conspirators. They spread rumors. They don't trust others. They're negative. They're fearful.

chapter three

Philadelphia Experiment

Theorists think the government did a secret experiment. This is the story: The government made an invisible ship. It did this in Philadelphia. It was in 1943. The ship was called the *Eldridge*. Scientists bent light around the ship. But something went wrong. There were blue lights. There was green fog. The ship was sent through time and space. It met aliens. It reappeared in a different city. It returned to Philadelphia. It went back 10 minutes in time. Some sailors got hurt. They melted into the ship. Some were turned inside out. Some disappeared. Survivors went crazy. Their minds were wiped clear. This is so they couldn't remember anything.

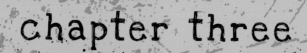

The U.S. Navy has denied doing any strange experiments.

chapter four

Kennedy Assassination

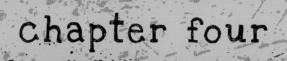

President John F. Kennedy was killed. This happened on November 22, 1963. Two bullets killed him. One bullet hit his head. Another bullet hit his neck. He was in Dallas, Texas. Lee Harvey Oswald was charged with the killing. He acted alone.

But that's not what theorists think. They think President Kennedy's death was a **plot**. Plots are secret plans. They think people were mad at the president. Some theorists think there was another gunman. Some blame **CIA** agents. The CIA is a government agency. Some blame the Soviets. Some blame a mysterious

14

Oswald was shot by Jack Ruby. Theorists think this was to silence Oswald.

man with a black umbrella. Some blame the mob. The mob
is an organized group of criminals.

chapter five

Lizard Lords

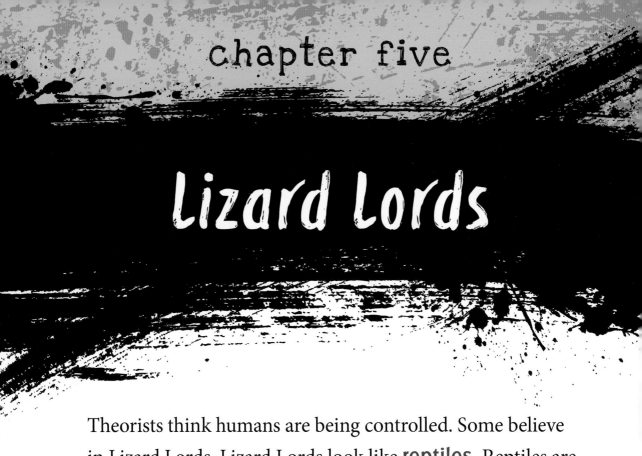

Theorists think humans are being controlled. Some believe in Lizard Lords. Lizard Lords look like **reptiles**. Reptiles are a type of animal. They have scaly skin.

Conspiracy theorists believe that Lizard Lords have ruled over humans since ancient times. They want to turn humans into slaves. They take on human shapes. But they can change shapes. They drink blood. They eat people. They're from outer space.

They pretend to be humans. They're our leaders. They're business owners. They're actors. They're singers. Theorists have

The Lizard Lords are also called the Reptilian Elite or "Annunaki."

accused many people of being Lizard Lords. Some say that Queen Elizabeth and Hillary Clinton are Lizard Lords.

Lizard Lords are among the world's most powerful people. They control the news. They control governments. They control religions. They're blamed for the world's troubles. They cause wars. They cause bombings. They cause sicknesses.

David Icke is the main theorist of this conspiracy. He has written books about Lizard Lords. He calls the British royal family "reptiles with crowns." He has guessed the end of the world. He says alien reptiles created humans. He says Lizard Lords were creating a "new world order."

Lizard people have shown up in folktales.

Spotlight Biography

Linda Moulton Howe was born in 1942. She was born in Idaho. She was Miss Idaho. She has a master's degree from Stanford University. She's an investigative journalist. This means she does research and writes articles. She also makes films. She studies the environment. She studies UFOs. UFOS are unidentified flying objects. They're thought to be alien spacecraft. She believes in many conspiracy theories. She believes the U.S. government is working with aliens. She believes cattle wounds are caused by aliens. She believes crop circles are caused by aliens. She believes that aliens have kidnapped people. She said, "I am convinced that one or more alien intelligences are affecting this planet."

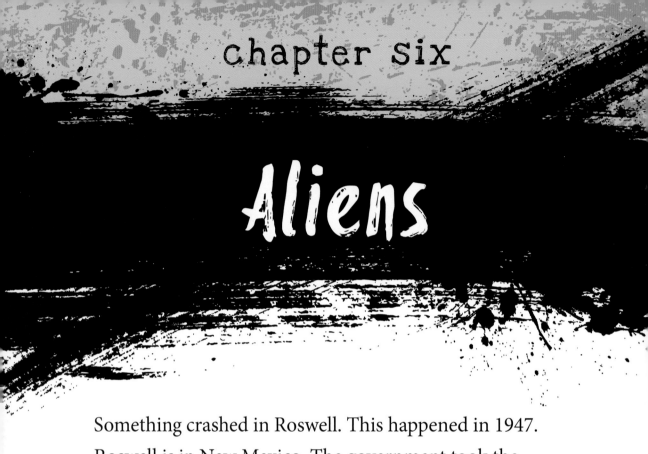

chapter six

Aliens

Something crashed in Roswell. This happened in 1947. Roswell is in New Mexico. The government took the wreckage. It said the crash was a weather balloon.

But conspiracy theorists don't believe it. Charles Berlitz and William Moore studied Roswell. They interviewed over 90 people. They think an alien spaceship flew over New Mexico. Then it got hit by lightning. This killed the aliens. The government pulled away dead aliens. It got rid of the spaceship. It added weather balloon scraps instead. Theorists think the government uses alien power to make weapons.

The government says the "alien bodies" are really crash test dummies. Dummies are fake bodies.

chapter seven

Flat-Earthers

Flat-Earthers think the Earth is flat. They think there's a **dome** over Earth. Domes are shaped like bowls. Flat-Earthers think stars are holes in the dome. They think Earth is a disc. They think the sun and moon move over the Earth. They think the Arctic Circle is the center. They think Antarctica is a tall wall of ice. The wall is around the edges of the disc. Going over the wall leads to falling off.

Theorists don't believe the photos from space. These photos show Earth as a **sphere**. Spheres are balls. Flat-Earthers think the photos are fake.

Flat-Earthers don't believe in gravity.

chapter eight

Chemtrails

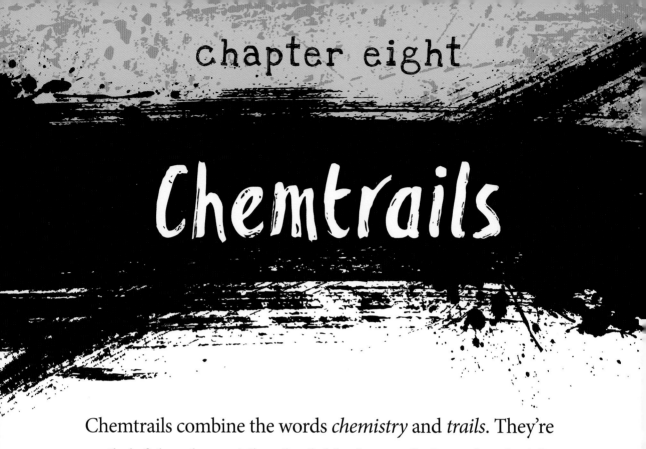

Chemtrails combine the words *chemistry* and *trails*. They're trails left by planes. They look like lines of white clouds. They stay for a while. They don't disappear like other plane trails.

Theorists think the trails are evil. The government is thought to be spraying chemicals. It sprays bad things for people to breathe. It controls people's minds. The government causes sickness. This is how it controls the human population. It controls the weather. It tests weapons.

Some theorists think chemtrails are used to hide another planet.

24

The trails are streaks created by gas from a plane's engine combined with low temperatures.

chapter nine

Holocaust

The **Holocaust** happened during World War II. Adolf Hitler was the leader of Nazi Germany. He killed at least 6 million Jews. It was a terrible time.

There are people who deny the Holocaust. They agree that Jews were sent to prison camps. But they think Hitler just wanted to **deport** Jews. Deport means to send to another country.

They don't think Hitler wanted to kill Jews. They don't think many Jews died. They think people made up the Holocaust. They think gas rooms were just **rumors**. Rumors are fake news.

Holocaust deniers say it didn't happen. They're wrong.

There's proof for the Holocaust. Germany even **apologized**. Apologizing means saying you're sorry. But conspiracy theorists have their own ideas.

chapter ten

Moon Landings

Neil Armstrong and Buzz Aldrin stepped on the moon.
They were the first two humans to do this. They were on
Apollo 11. This was a spacecraft. It launched in 1969. After
that, there were six more moon landings. Twelve
astronauts have been on the moon. Astronauts are pilots.
They fly to space.

But theorists think the moon landings were all faked. The
"space race" was a competition. It was
between the United States and Russia.
Theorists think the U.S. lied. The U.S.
wanted to beat Russia. Armstrong and

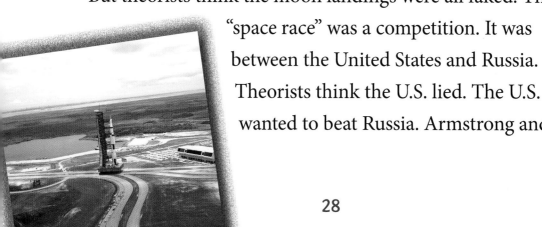

Theorists think Stanley Kubrick helped NASA. Kubrick makes movies. He made 2001: A Space Odyssey.

Aldrin were thought to be actors. NASA made a secret film set. They took fake photos of the moon.

Theorists don't believe the photos. They question the shadows. They question the lack of stars. They question the moon rocks. Theorists think the government killed some astronauts. It did this to keep them quiet.

Aldrin put a flag on the moon. Theorists say the flag moved. They think there was wind. But there's no wind in space. NASA says Aldrin was twisting the pole into moon soil. This made the flag move.

Some theorists blame NASA. NASA is thought to have used the fake landings to make money. Some theorists blame the government. The government is thought to have used the fake landings to distract people.

Theorists think Buzz Aldrin was part of the conspiracy.

Try This!

- Think about an event that is happening right now. Create your own conspiracy theory about the event. Tell people about your theory. See if they believe you.

- Go to museums. Look for evidence to prove conspiracy theorists wrong. For example, go to the Museum of Tolerance in Los Angeles, California. See the evidence for the Holocaust.

- Talk to people who believe in conspiracy theories. Ask questions. Find out what they're thinking.

- Go to the library. Do internet research. Learn about other conspiracy theories.

- Read the news. Use your critical-thinking skills. Decide if it's good or bad information.

Consider This!

Take a Position! Choose one of the conspiracy theories described in this book. Do more research about it. Do you think there's any truth to the theory? Do you think it's valid or not? Argue your point with reasons and evidence.

Say What? There are many conspiracy theories. How do they get started? Why do people believe in conspiracy theories? Create your own conspiracy theory. Explain your idea.

Think About It! There's been a lot of talk about "alternative facts." What are "alternative facts"? How are conspiracy theories similar to "alternative facts"? How are they different?

Learn More!

- Meltzer, Brad, and Keith Ferrell. *History Decoded: The 10 Greatest Conspiracies of All Time*. New York: Workman Publishing Company, 2013.
- Samuels, Charlie. *Conspiracy!* New York: Crabtree Publishing Company, 2013.

Glossary

apologized (uh-PAH-luh-jized) said "sorry"

astronauts (AS-truh-nawts) people who travel to space

CIA (SEE EYE A) stands for Central Intelligence Agency, responsible for U.S. national security

communists (KAHM-yuh-nists) people who believe property and goods should be owned in common and distributed as needed

conspiracy (kuhn-SPIR-uh-see) secret plans

decay (dih-KAY) rot

deport (dih-PORT) to send to another country

dome (DOHM) a bowl-shaped roof or ceiling

fluoride (FLOR-ide) mineral used to prevent tooth decay

Holocaust (HAH-luh-kawst) the organized killing of Jewish people by Nazi Germany as led by Adolf Hitler

mob (MAHB) an organized group of criminals

plot (PLAHT) secret plan

reptiles (REP-tilez) types of animals that have scaly skin and are cold-blooded

rumors (ROO-murz) fake news, gossip, or stories that aren't true

sphere (SFEER) ball

theories (THEER-eez) ideas

theorists (THEER-ists) people who believe in theories

witness (WIT-nis) a person who sees something happening

Index